a month of magic

30-Day Poetry Journal
with samples, guides, and prompts

r.c. perez

Copyright © 2022 r.c. perez

All rights reserved. This book or any portion thereof may not be reproduced or used in any manner whatsoever without the express written permission of the publisher except for the use of brief quotations in a book review and certain other noncommercial uses permitted by copyright law.

ISBN: 978-1-7776334-2-4 (Print)

Fonts and graphics from Canva
Poem illustrations by Angela Dianne Agustin
Cover design template by SelfPubMagic on Etsy

ignovionwrites@gmail.com
@ignovionwrites

This Journal Belongs To:
_____

how to use this journal

Dear writer,

Welcome!

So, you've taken on the challenge to write a poem each day for 30 days. That is quite admirable! If you are a beginner writer wishing to improve your craft or if you have been writing for a while and looking for new inspiration for writing, this poetry journal is perfect for you.

What you will find in this journal:

Sample Poems. Each task begins with a poem from my poetry collection **magic of the modest**. The poems serve as examples from which the prompts will be based.

Explanation/Guide. Following each poem is a section that describes the process that went behind writing it while explaining some basic concepts and techniques in writing poetry or offering general insights to topics related to writing.

Writing Prompts. Finally, a writing prompt will be provided which will challenge you to apply the concepts discussed in the previous section. The prompts vary in format and complexity. Some prompts will require you to write a specific type of poem while some are open-ended questions that invite you to ponder on and write a poem about.

This poetry journal will help you:

- ❖ Develop your own style
- ❖ Discover your own voice
- ❖ Find your niche
- ❖ Practice some of the most useful poetic techniques
- ❖ Gain a lot of insights about writing

After a month, you will have produced 30 new poems and by then, I hope you would have found the experience "magical".

Regardless of your motivation for using this poetry journal, I hope that you will find this book helpful and that you will come out with more appreciation for poetry and an invigorated soul to motivate you to keep writing.

Best of luck and always stay magical!

r.c. perez

And it was at this age... Poetry arrived in search of me

Pablo Neruda

I

Fire—
your eyes,
warm and wild.
May you never lose
the wonder of a child.

TEMPLATE POEMS

As a middle school/high school teacher, I am very aware of the impression that poetry is difficult. Very often when students come to the classroom, they have already decided that poetry is not for them, but I found out that most of the time, they just don't know where to start.

I have since then figured out that when it comes to writing poetry, an effective way is to start with template poems (poems that have specific guidelines on the format), such as cinquains, acrostics, and haikus. Template poems are great because they take away the intimidation that comes from not knowing where to start or what to write about.

For your first prompt, write a poem similar to the example on the previous page.

The template: 5 lines; the first line has one word (your subject/topic), second line has two words, third line has three words, and so on.

PROMPT #1

Write a template poem of the same format as the example.

Some suggestions for the first word (feel free to come up with your own):

| sunrise | river | fireflies |
| growth | power | dreams |

I promise,
all days before me
will become faded memory
of a time you didn't know love.

WORD PROMPTS

Responding to word prompts is a good exercise to get yourself into writing a poem, especially if you're having one of those days when you can't seem to find inspiration.

As a poet who started on Instagram, I thrived from participating in word prompt challenges. Surprisingly, some of my finest poems (in my opinion) are products of these challenges.

Originality is very important in art, so how I approach word prompts is that I try to be unexpected. I try to find another layer in a given prompt, take its alternate meaning and work on it, or completely turn it around and give it a twist. For example, the previous poem is one I wrote on the prompt "faded memory." My first instinct was to write a sad poem, but I realized everybody was probably going to write a sad poem, so I thought about how to use the prompt to write a poem that is more positive or hopeful.

Today, try your hand at writing a poem out of a word prompt.

PROMPT #2

Write a short poem on **ONE** *of the following words. Be unexpected.*

candlelight	mirror	blanket
bonfire	regret	abandon

The Falling

Day by day
piece by piece
slowly, soundlessly
like a tree shedding leaves
I fall for you.

SIMILES AND METAPHORS

One of the most common poetic techniques used by poets is a simile or a metaphor. Both of them are used for comparisons, but the main difference is that simile uses the words "as" or "like" when comparing, whereas metaphor uses direct comparison by saying that one is the other.

A big part of the appeal of poetry comes from the creative use of language. **"Show, don't tell"** is perhaps the most basic rule of creative writing. There are many ways to do this, and being descriptive through the use of similes and metaphors is one.

Today's prompt is an exercise on being descriptive by using simile or metaphor.

PROMPT #3

Write a short poem that makes use of simile or metaphor.

Strength,

if you are
a thing that flows,
let it be water
that hollows out
a stone—

drop by drop,
calm, and
constant.

INTANGIBLES

Poets often deal with intangible and abstract ideas, such as love, longing, and courage. Good writers have a way of presenting these topics to make them more concrete and easily understood by readers without sacrificing creativity.

The example poem takes inspiration from Ocean Vuong. Another poet, William Bortz, wrote a poem with a similar structure.

I fell in love with this structure because, with it, something abstract becomes concrete by comparing it with something rather unexpected but still makes sense. I was able to write four poems as a result.

For Prompt #4, you are challenged to talk about an abstract idea and present it in a more concrete way.

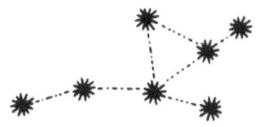

PROMPT #4

Write a poem of the same format as the example (i.e. _____, if you are _____, let it be _____).
Some topic suggestions (feel free to come up with your own):

humility	healing	success
death	laughter	forgiveness

Skin Hunger

But our fingers are made
to brush against
somebody else's skin.
These arms of ours
are meant for long
and warm embrace.

Take me back to the time
when it wasn't sin
to hunger for skin.

COVID CHRONICLES

Because poetry often reflects the realities at the time it is written, it can serve as a window from which we can see how the people at a certain period in history lived. Sure, history books can give us that information but with poetry, we get a clearer understanding of how people thought, felt about, and processed the things happening around them. In other words, we get to see the "human" side of events in history.

We are at a very interesting point in history right now as we slowly start coming out from the pandemic that caused deaths and affected livelihoods, among other devastating effects. We are eyewitnesses to unprecedented times.

A hundred years from now, people will read literature about the COVID-19 pandemic to understand how it is to live in the time of face masks and social distancing.

What then, would you like them to know?

PROMPT #5

Write a pandemic poem — a poem that explores your thoughts, feelings, and experiences related to the COVID-19 pandemic.

Biopic

*Spoiler—
we die in the end.*
So what?
Play your life, anyway
—play it loud, do not
skip even just
one second of it.
There is no rewind.

Pause if ....

it gets too much,
and then, resume.
Enjoy it; stay put
for the credits.
Take a look, one last time,
at the cast that made
your blockbuster
of a life possible,
all the people
you are thankful for.

TRANSFORMATIVE ART

The previous poem is a response to a prompt on Instagram to write a poem that starts with the line "Spoiler—we die in the end" by the poet Atticus. I wrote a poem that builds on this line and explored my thoughts about knowing that one day I will die (like it is any surprise at all).

Today, try to transform the first line of "The Love Song of J. Alfred Prufrock" into something new.

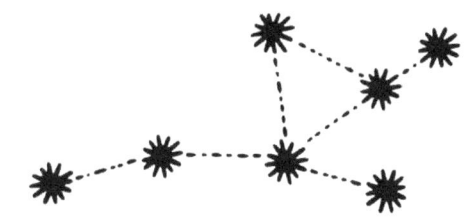

PROMPT #6

Write a poem that begins with the following line:

"Let us go then, you and I"

Parade of Leaves

In the faintest yellows
I saw gentle surrender,
in the brightest reds
I saw burning hope.
And somewhere in
between, a simple truth:
for every leaf that falls,
something new
is coming along.

POETRY IN NATURE

Nature has inspired poets for thousands of years, and it's easy to understand why. It is full of wisdom and beauty, and any keen observer can turn into a poet from a mere encounter with nature.

Some writers have suggested that a quick nature walk is a good remedy for writer's block, and it makes sense because not only is nature an opportunity to clear one's mind but it also provides a writer with countless ideas to write about.

From William Wordsworth's "I Wandered Lonely as a Cloud" to Mary Oliver's "The Kingfisher", it can be argued that **some of the most enduring poems are poems about nature**. They have timeless and universal appeal.

Today, you are encouraged to be with nature and simply observe its wisdom and beauty.

PROMPT #7

Write a poem inspired by one of your observations of nature.

So many lives
I couldn't live;
so many worlds
I will never see.

Give me poetry.
Let me in;
let me *be*.

WHY POETRY?

You are using this journal because poetry means something to you, whether you are just starting to appreciate poetry and want to improve, or you have been writing for a while now and want to find new inspiration for writing.

Poets will always give you different answers to the question about the meaning of poetry and why they write. To many, it is a creative outlet; to others, it is a way to understand the world. Some write poetry to navigate their emotions while others write poetry to inspire.

Why do you write poetry?
What does poetry mean to you?

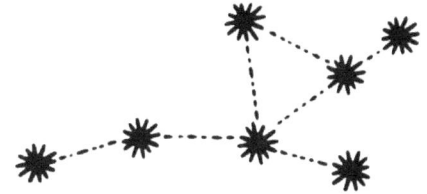

PROMPT #8

Write a poem that explores what poetry means to you.

Wednesday

My name is Wednesday,
not the beginning
nor the end.
I am just here
and you might take
me for granted.

But if you ever find me,
please do not look back—
you have come so far.
Do not look too far ahead—
it is still a long way.
Savor me and all
that I can offer.

I am the calm
in the midst
of all this chaos.

Today, you are exactly
where you need to be.

SKY'S THE LIMIT

So, what do poets write about again?

Everything and anything.

Poetry is arguably the **most creative form of literature**, primarily because of the emphasis it gives on language—use of poetic sound devices and figures of speech, careful and deliberate choice of words, sentence structure—all to convey a message or invoke emotions in very condensed form.

But poetry is also creative in that it can present perhaps any topic or subject, even the most mundane, everyday objects in a beautiful, thought-provoking, or inspiring way.

Pablo Neruda, for example, wrote a poem about an onion! Safe to say, a poet should never run out of things to write about.

PROMPT #9

Pick one of the days of the week and make it the subject of your poem.

(Alternatively, pick one of the months and make it your subject.)

The Magic of True Friendship

Years
and oceans
apart,
and so much
life in between.

But I know
no matter how far,
no matter how long,
I could talk to you
again, as though
not a day went by.

CONNECTIONS

How do you measure friendship? How do you know if someone is a true friend?

Technology has presumably brought everyone together, but I feel like it has become even more difficult to find real and deep connections these days. While it is true that it is so easy to connect to anyone using social media, it is also very easy to disconnect. It is a curse, in my opinion, that for the most part, the relationships we end up building with people are too often, very surface-level.

I'm sure most of us have already realized that just because we talk to someone every day doesn't mean they are our friends. And then, there are people whom we rarely talk to, but we know deep inside they are our friends. I define true friendship simply as being able to talk to someone even after a long time being apart or not talking and it is as if not a day went by—no awkwardness, no hesitations, no judgments. I call it the magic of true friendship.

What is your idea of friendship?

PROMPT #10

Write a poem that expresses your thoughts on the "magic" of true friendship

II

Things I Missed

The blue night bus, one cold North York
November night. The chance to ask for
the stranger's name, at the stop. The alarm.
Early morning classes. The fun. That time
somebody probably said, *This is already the
best days of our lives.* Calls. Shots I didn't take.
Half of my life. Whatever *never mind* really
meant. Opportunities to speak up. A beat.
The point. Punchlines. Deadlines. Subtle
hints. Easter eggs. Freeway exits, because
I always drive and daydream. The target.
Many, many chances at love.

EXPERIMENTAL POETRY

According to Anne Huang, **experimental poetry** is a type of poetry that emphasizes innovation. Poets who write experimental poetry veer away from the traditional standards of form and look for new ways to present words and convey meaning.

e.e. cummings' "l(a" is perhaps one of the prime examples of experimental poetry that completely disregards conventions.

Because experimental poetry breaks the rules, the poet is free to create their own, or as Anne Huang puts it, to have an "alternative engagement with convention."

Experiment with your next poem by thinking of an alternative way to write it.

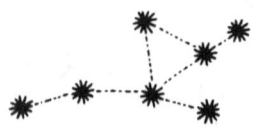

Pick one title to write a poem about:

    Things I Missed
    Things I Broke
    Things I Held

Recipe for Hope

one cup
a spoonful
one sip
a smile at the void
two shots
one spirited sigh

If only we could measure hope,
if only the heart knows limits, if only.
This is what the break of day looks,
when coffee tastes marvelous
and hope overflows.

POETRY AS EXPLORATION

The previous poem started as an attempt to recreate the format of an activity I often use in my class. It's called Symbolic Recipe, in which students are asked to introduce themselves by presenting themselves as recipes, with their qualities and traits as ingredients.

I wanted to apply it to explore what constitutes hope, but in the process, my writing took a bit of a different direction from what I originally planned. This happens a lot when writing poetry because the truth is, too often when poets sit down to write, they have no idea how their poem is going to look like in the end. **Poetry is essentially a process of exploration and discovery.**

Try it with today's prompt. Start with a given format, but don't be afraid to divert if a better idea comes up. See what you can come up with in the end.

PROMPT #12

Write your own "Recipe for" poem. Pick one below or come up with your own.

strength inner peace

 confidence

Sound of Love

If someday
somebody asks,
*What sound
did it make for you,
the falling in love?*

I will smile and say,
I used to think
it would be a loud
thumping of the heart,
but it was the crackle
of leaves being crushed
by two pairs of feet
walking side by side.

APPEAL TO SENSES

Imagery in poetry is defined as a description that appeals to the reader's senses and imagination. In other words, if you can clearly picture or imagine the scene in a poem, that's imagery.

Many people think that imagery is all about the sense of sight; but descriptions that make you imagine how a certain object smells or sounds, for example, are also imagery.

Imagery is a powerful tool in a poet's toolbox. A poet who effectively uses imagery makes readers feel something, which is what good poetry should do. It allows the readers to connect with the poem and easily understand its meaning because abstract ideas become more concrete.

Today, challenge yourself by writing a poem that relies heavily on the use of imagery, particularly, the sense of hearing.

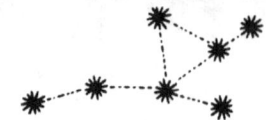

PROMPT #13

What is the sound of love?

Last

One last time—
you, tonight with me,
and tomorrow,
a memory.

SHORT AND SWEET

One of the most common questions about writing poetry is how long a poem should be. Well, it can be short, it can be long. In fact, it can be of any length (think epic poems).

I am drawn to very short poems. To me, there is just so much beauty and art in being able to say so much in very few words. And that's precisely why it is very challenging to write short poems, far harder than writing longer poems. It takes **mastery and precision with words** to be able to do that.

Emily Dickinson and e. e. cummings are known for writing very short poems. And while we can never in this lifetime be like them, we can at least try.

Yes, we try.

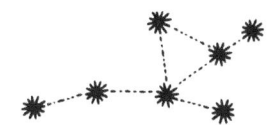

PROMPT #14

Write an 11-word poem.

Aguinaldo

There was a time of innocence,
of dreams, and of simple things.
There was a time when all we had
and all we could give was bliss.

Sixteen years gone
and didn't time just fly by?
I will speak of you not as a father
but as a child—
chubby cheeks, clad in your best clothes,
hair neatly combed
—a split second when life was perfect,
forever frozen in that faded photograph.

A POEM FOR YOU

And which poet didn't write a poem about or for someone?

Poets spend their whole lives trying to find the right words to tell people in their lives how they feel about them, whether they be lovers, friends, family, or even a stranger on the street.

Consider yourself special if someone wrote a poem about you. There is a saying that goes, "if you want to live forever, love a poet because they will immortalize you in their poems."

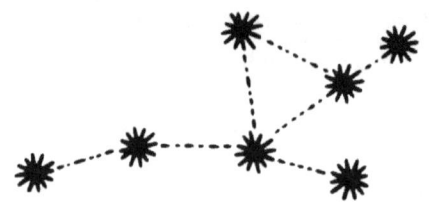

 PROMPT #15

Write a poem about a person in your life.

Sunshine

Sunshine smile
and sparkly eyes—
how could you
possibly hold
that much light?

When you walk around
with all your warmth,
I feel it in my skin
and I swear,
I could not
be more alive.

WORD PROMPT PART 2

The previous poem is another example of a poem I wrote out of a word prompt—sunshine. I like word prompts because it challenges a writer to think outside the box, to render a new meaning or interpretation of an otherwise very simple or common word.

Today, challenge yourself by working on a word prompt that is equally common—blush.

What makes you blush?

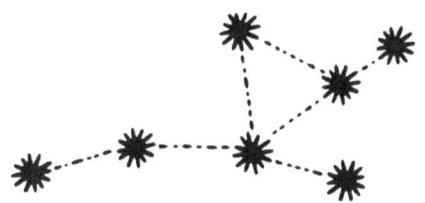

PROMPT #16

Write a poem on
"BLUSH"

A Place

Why is it
that we may hang our coats
and still not call it home?

Why is it
that we may sit around the table,
laugh at each other's jokes
and still feel alone?

There must be a place
where we belong.
This can't be
all there is.

HOME

What is a home? Where is home? Is it a place? Is it a person? How do you know if you have found it?

As a poet, these are some of the many questions I have tried to find answers to, through my poetry. Even now I am still constantly navigating through the idea of "home" and many poems later, I still haven't found a satisfying answer.

But one thing I have found out is that many of us are looking for that one place where we can say we belong. I guess at the end of the day, we're all lost and just trying to find *home*, whatever that may mean for us.

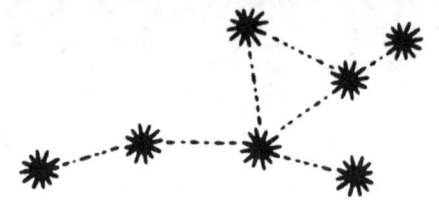

PROMPT #17

What does home look like to you?

Shell

I picked up a shell on the shore
hoping to hear your voice inside,

because I once read somewhere,
those who loved and were loved
never really die—
they come back as magic,

because I am learning
there is no longing
quite as painful
as missing the sound
of your laughter in the flesh.

ON GRIEF

Grief has many faces. It manifests in different ways. We deal with it in different ways. Sometimes, we mistake it for anger; too often it hides behind smiles rather than tears.

Death is not the only loss we grieve for. We grieve for lost friendships and love, for dreams that didn't come true, for the people we once were.

Loss is a reality of life. And so is grief. Today, reflect on this feeling that is all too familiar to every one of us.

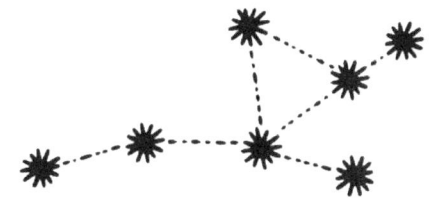

PROMPT #18

Write a poem about grief.

The One Who Wonders

I had a thought,
a wild and wondrous one,
that somewhere far off
there is a place
where what the heart speaks
is echoed by the mind.

Imagine bliss,
imagine freedom.

I had this thought,
and it may very well be
just a wishful, whimsical one.

But if by chance
you come across a wanderer
who knows the way
to this wonderland,
would you be kind enough
to tell them about a dreamer
whose only wish is to fly?

ALLITERATION

How a poem sounds when read aloud is just as important as how it appears on paper, if not more important. After all, poems are traditionally meant to be recited out loud, and in some cultures, even sung.

It is important for a poet, therefore, to pay attention to the use of words that will bring out the musical quality of language.

Using poetic sound devices is one technique to achieve this. **Alliteration**, or when a poet uses words that start with the same sound close to each other, is one of the most used poetic sound devices. Alliteration helps a poem "sound good" by making sentences easily roll off the tongue, so to speak. For instance, the phrase "wild and wondrous one" uses the "W" sound for the three words.

Today, try to write a poem that uses alliteration. Afterward, read your poem out loud and see for yourself.

PROMPT #19

Write a poem that uses alliteration.

The Existence

If a tree falls in a forest
and I am the only one
around to hear it,
I hope I will remember
what sound it makes,
so I could tell everyone
it did, indeed, exist

PHILOSOPHY AND POETRY

To some, philosophy and poetry exist in separate spheres. That is if we consider that philosophy is mainly concerned with logic and reasoning while poetry is all about emotions and expression. But a lot of philosophy is also about finding truth and meaning. And isn't that also what poetry is about? Poetry often explores concepts of existence and the meaning of life and seeks to find answers to life's biggest questions.

It can be argued then, that philosophy can be expressed through poetry. Or further, that **philosophy inspires poetry**. Sometimes, poets even use poetry to explore their relationships and understanding of some philosophical arguments or concepts.

Today, you are challenged to interpret a philosophical statement and write a poem about it.

PROMPT #20

Explore Leibniz' statement and write a poem reimagining or interpreting it.

"We live in the best of all possible worlds."

III

Smile, you're doing great so far. 😊

Tawhay

I hang my keys on the wall as I get home,
take off my shoes, undress myself from Today,
wash all What Could Have Beens off my skin,
and put on a pair of plain, simple What Is.
I am learning to be comfortable sleeping in them.

BEAUTIFUL WORDS

Tawhay, in the Hiligaynon language of the Philippines, is a concept that refers to the state of being relaxed, at peace, and without worry.

There are similar terms in the English language, such as *inner peace*, but none, in my opinion, quite captures the essence of the word.

There are many beautiful concepts and words in different languages whose meaning and essence are untranslatable. And that's where the beauty of these words comes from. They are "poetic" all on their own.

If you speak a language other than English, can you think of a word/concept that you find beautiful that cannot be fully translated?

Alternatively, what word in the English language do you find most beautiful?

 **PROMPT #21**

Write a poem about a beautiful word/concept in your language.

Sunshower

I want to be out
in a sunshower with you,
stare at you
under the glitter waterfall.

I'd take you to the woods.
Cold and drenched,
we'll find a procession—
a wedding of beasts.

This, I'd say, and ours,
is the romance
this summer rain brings.

STORIES

Once, while researching about cultural universals, I stumbled upon a write-up about how almost all cultures in the world have folklore about sunshowers, and although there are some variations, one common theme is that according to the stories, when the sun is out while the rain is pouring, some animal or mystical creatures are getting married.

In the Philippines, for example, it's the *Tikbalang*—a half-human, half-horse creature.

I was so fascinated by this and thought that sunshowers must be so romantic and mystical that even the animals, all over the world, would want to get married.

How about in your culture? Do you have similar beliefs about sunshowers? What other folklores/legends/superstitions in your culture fascinate you?

PROMPT #22

Write a poem about a folklore/ legend/ superstitious belief in your culture that fascinates you.

Turns

When I am frail
I know
you will be strong.
When you find it
unbearable
I will carry it for you.

No, my love,
we do not make
each other strong.
We take turns
being strong
for each other.

Inside our embrace,
there is enough space
for weakness.

POINTS-OF-VIEW

Many of us have this idea of love as this great force that, all of a sudden, makes everything, or everyone, better. "You make me strong" is such a sweet sentiment from a person in love, isn't it? But while this sounds so romantic, I'm not sure if it is at all empowering. To me, it implies that one's strength is dependent on another person.

These are the thoughts I contemplated while writing the poem on the previous page. I wanted to figure out what I think of strength as it relates to love.

I think that loving someone so deeply allows a person to discover their true strength already inside of them in order to protect the person they love. But more importantly, love gives someone a space where they can be vulnerable and still feel safe.

But then again, this is just my own take, and it might be that a lot of people would disagree. That's the thing about poetry—**it doesn't just make you feel; it also makes you think**. Poetry allows a reader to see how a poet sees the world and then, reflect on their own viewpoints.

PROMPT #23

Write a poem about an opinion on a topic that might be considered a "hot take".

Dust

And if I were indeed
just a speck of dust,
infinitesimal
and irrelevant,

at least let me be
the kind that settles
on the windshield glass
where someone's fingers
will trace for the both of us,

words of quiet declaration,
perhaps in between sighs:

I was here.

LEGACY

As the saying goes, in the grand scheme of things, we are all just a speck of dust. I suppose this is disappointing for many of us because we are generally consumed by the idea of doing something great throughout our lives and leaving a legacy for generations to come.

Perhaps it is the height of human hubris. In reality, we might just be too scared to perish—to be forgotten when we die.

Not all of us are destined to do great things. But all of us can do small things—acts that make a difference in the lives of others, even for just one person. And what very little we can do, we should do, if only to prove we ever existed at all. Perhaps, in the end, that is our true legacy.

Today, contemplate on the "legacy" you want to leave behind.

PROMPT #24

How would you like to be remembered?

Another World

When things around you
get cold, remember,
there is another world.

Fly,
fly away from here.
Find all the warmth
and fill your heart with it.

CHANGES

In life, we sometimes get to a point where the things we do or the place we're at don't give us joy anymore. More popularly, this feeling of lack of enthusiasm for the things that used to be enjoyable is called "burnout".

When this happens, what we can do is reassess and recalibrate ourselves to discover what else is out there for us. Change is good. And because our passions, our priorities, our mindsets and worldviews change, we have to adapt and embrace change. The key, I think, is to always remind ourselves to go for what makes us feel alive—the things that give us warmth. A hobby? A sport? An adventure? A person? Whatever that is, don't be afraid to follow it.

For today's prompt, contemplate on "CHANGE" and write your ideas about it.

PROMPT #25

Write a poem about

CHANGE.

Magic of the Modest

Sometimes, it's simply the warmth
of your blanket and the softness
of your pillows at night.

Sometimes, it's a new pen, and you
could swear, you have never found
one that glided and wrote so well.

A cordial smile from a stranger;
a parcel; the way your hair looks
perfect today; cheesecake;
a childhood friend who stayed.

Oh, these little things
and all random, ordinary, joyful things
—gratitude, for all of them.

Meegwetch for the magic of the modest!

MAGIC

My collection of poetry, Magic of the Modest, is based on Roald Dahl's quote about the magic of simple things. It goes, "And above all, watch with glittering eyes the whole world around you because the greatest secrets are always hidden in the most unlikely places."

Truly there is joy hidden behind the ordinary and the mundane, and if we just look close enough, we will see it. Today, I invite you to reflect on the simple things that give you joy. Make a list of them and write a poem expressing your thoughts and feelings about the magic of the modest.

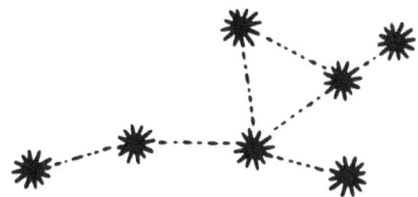

PROMPT #26

Write a poem about the simple things that give you joy.

A Life Lived

If I'm lucky enough
to reach the autumn
of my life, I wish
that each falling leaf
be a photograph—
a snapshot of a life
lived not in dullness
but in all colors bright.

And when all is done,
there will be nothing
left of me.
But wasn't that beautiful?
someone will proclaim
with their glittering eyes.

It was. It really was.

TO LIVE

How can you say that you have actually truly lived?

Life and death are perennial topics poets explore and for many of us, death is such a tragedy. But death is one of the very few certainties in this world. And I have always wondered, on my death bed, what will I be thinking when my time has come? When I look back at my life, will I be happy and satisfied? I hope I will be. Too often, we are so afraid to die that we forget to live. And to live it beautifully.

What, to you, is a beautiful life?

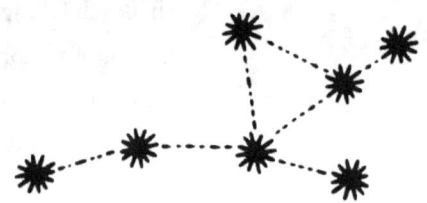

PROMPT #27

What is a beautiful life?

Acceptance Speech

Today,
above all things,
I accept
who I am
and all
the greatness
within me.

ENOUGH, WORTHY, CAPABLE

One of the most freeing acts in life is to accept yourself for who you are—to come to terms with your imperfections, your mistakes, and limitations, but more importantly, to recognize the great things you are capable of.

I wrote this short piece at a time when I needed to tell myself that I am worthy, regardless. But I also wanted it to be something that someone will stumble upon somewhere and will inspire them to take their own journey towards self-acceptance.

Today, I invite you to expand this poem by listing down specific things about yourself that you are finally willing to accept. List down the things that have kept your self-confidence low all this time. But I also want you to list down the great things about you that you have been very hesitant to acknowledge, for whatever reason. Consider this prompt as an exercise in freeing yourself from the idea that you are not enough, worthy, and capable.

PROMPT #28

Write your own "Acceptance Speech" poem.

In the Phone Booth

I think I can't thank
the rain enough
for drowning the sound
of my pounding heart.

In the phone booth,
that afternoon we were alone,
I had no excuse
if you asked me what
the jitter was all about.

BE SPECIFIC

Sometimes, poets talk about experiences that are very personal or specific to them. When good poets do this, they provide us with very specific details, objects, places, or situations, and one might think that it will make the poem unrelatable. Yet these kinds of poems are actually the ones that are most memorable and compelling for the exact reason that they are very specific.

Specificity helps with effective storytelling and builds authenticity. A poem that talks about something very general does not affect the reader as much as a specific poem does because, in the latter, the reader is convinced it is something the author has truly experienced.

For today's prompt, you will write a poem about a special place. The challenge is to describe it in a personal, specific way.

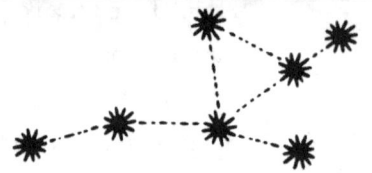

PROMPT #29

Write a poem about a special place.

Covenants

And he said to him,
Your love for me is wonderful;
your soul is knit to mine.
He armored him
with his own.
He loved him as himself.

And she said to her,
Where you go I will go,
and where you stay I will stay.
She cleaved unto her
like Adam clung to Eve.
Her home became her home.

If there is God
who invented love,
or is love, Himself,
then he must also be
the god of souls knit
and bodies cleaving
unto each other.

THE POWER TO EMPOWER

Poetry has always had a deep connection with the long history of resistance and social movements. It has been used to enlighten and empower people to become agents of change.

In today's society where important social movements are gaining necessary attention, such as Black Lives Matter, Me Too, mental health, Indigenous rights, and environmental protection, poets play a critical role in raising awareness, speaking truth, and encouraging people to participate in such causes.

For your final prompt, think about one cause or a social issue you are passionate about. As a poet, how would you like to be part of this movement? What would you like people to know? How would you like to empower them?

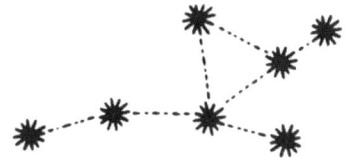

Write a poem about a social issue or a cause that you are passionate about.

CONGRATULATIONS ON FINISHING THIS JOURNAL!

What's next?

Edit your poems. You have 30 new poems all in one place. That's really great! But most likely, they still need some polishing. Give them a few days to rest. Then go back and edit. Proofread. Have a trusted person read them for feedback. Revise and finalize.

Read more poetry. Continue improving. The best way is to keep writing, but also, keep reading. Actively seek new kinds of poems to read and new poets to discover and admire.

Put your work out there. There is nothing to lose, but everything to gain. Social media is great to establish connections. Share your work online. You never know what may happen if you open yourself up to possibilities.

Stay magical.

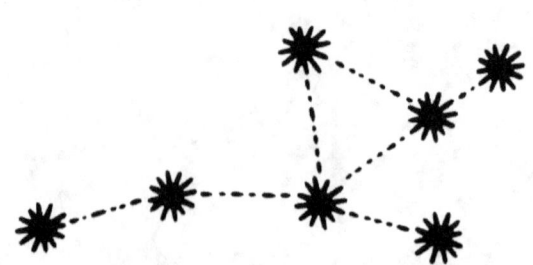

acknowlegments/references

The explanation of experimental poetry is guided by Ann Huang's article "What is Experimental Poetry & What Does It Mean?" on her website annhuang.com

The discussion on "Poetry and Philosophy" is guided by a conversation available on philosophytalk.org titled "Love, Poetry, and Philosophy"

The discussion on "The Power to Empower" is guided by an article on poetryfoundation.org titled "Poems of Protest, Resistance, and Empowerment"

Thank you to my laptop, which kept dying on me while finishing this project. Thanks for hanging in there.

about the author

r.c. perez is a Filipino-Canadian poet and teacher. He is the author of the poetry collection **magic of the modest**. In this journal, he combines his passions for poetry and education to offer a unique experience to writers looking for fresh inspiration. He lives in Toronto where he spends his free time geeking out on Ancient Egypt. He is currently working on his second poetry collection. Find him on Instagram (@ignovionwrites).

www.ingramcontent.com/pod-product-compliance
Lightning Source LLC
Chambersburg PA
CBHW072206100526
44589CB00015B/2386